Contents

Special Features

Features

Victoria's Vegetables

Written by Pierre Latour
Illustrated by Kelvin Hawley

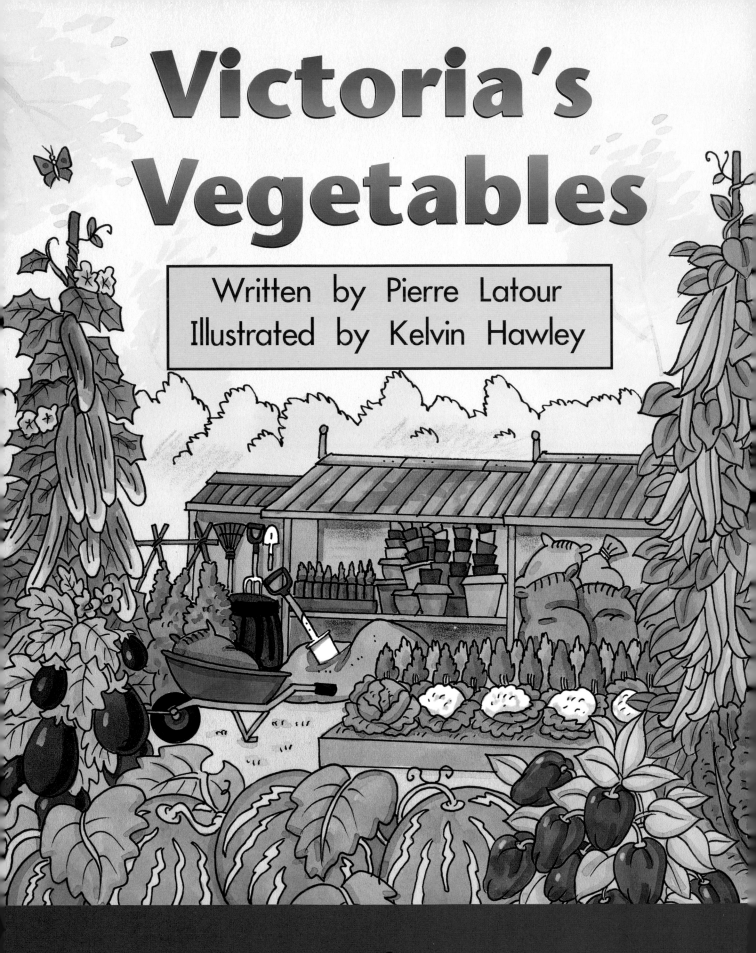

Victoria grew vegetables.
She grew vegetables that were big.
She grew vegetables that were long.

She grew vegetables that were green, and vegetables that were orange, and she grew vegetables that were purple.

A man came to
Victoria's vegetable garden.

"I want some vegetables,"
said the man.

"I have vegetables that are big, and vegetables that are long," said Victoria.
"I have vegetables that are green, and vegetables that are orange, and vegetables that are purple."

"Purple!" said the man.
"Vegetables are not purple!"

"This vegetable is purple,"
said Victoria.
"This vegetable is an eggplant."

"An eggplant," said the man. "An egg is not a vegetable. So an eggplant is not a vegetable."

"An eggplant is a vegetable," said Victoria.
"And it is purple!"

Safari
WORD POWER

 Zz

 Aa
 Yy

 Bb
 Xx

 Cc

 Dd
 Ww

 Ee
 Vv

 Ff
 Uu

 Gg

 Tt

 Hh
 Ss

Ii
 Rr

purple   some   butterfly

come   spider

garden   are

grew

Find –
are butterfly come garden
grew purple some spider

Jj   Kk   Ll   Mm   Nn   Oo   Pp   Qq

10

Come into the Garden

Written by Shirley-May Sweetman

Illustrated by Jim Storey

Come into the garden,
Don't get wet.
I have a spider
for a garden pet.

Come into the garden,
Don't get wet.
I have a butterfly
for a garden pet.

Come into the garden,
Don't get wet.
I have a grasshopper
for a garden pet.

bet
get
jet
met
net
pet
set
vet
wet
yet

Make a Kitchen Garden

Written by Cory Winesap
Photographed by Greg Brookes

You can make a garden
in your kitchen.
You can grow herbs
in your kitchen garden.

What You Will Need

Herb plants

Water

Soil

Pot

Saucer

What to do

1 Put the pot in the saucer.
Put the soil in the pot.

2 Make a little hole for the herb.

3 Put the herb in the little hole.
Pat the soil around the herb.

4 Water the herb.

These are some herbs that you can grow.

Basil

Thyme

Parsley

Chives

The Garden Party

Written by Sonny Reuben

Illustrated by Kelvin Hawley

Beetle

Butterfly

Bee

Caterpillar

Spider

Beetle

I am having a party. Will you come?

Caterpillar

I cannot come today.
I am eating a lettuce leaf.
I can come tomorrow.
Tomorrow I will bring a lettuce leaf for the party.

Spider

I cannot come today.
I am spinning a web.
I can come tomorrow.
Tomorrow I will bring a fly for the party.

Bee

I cannot come today.
I am getting nectar.
I can come tomorrow.
Tomorrow I will bring some nectar for the party.

Butterfly

I can come. I will help you with the party.

Beetle

I will have my party tomorrow.
Butterfly will help me with the party.

Caterpillar

Creep, creep, creep.
Here is the lettuce leaf
for the party.

Spider

Spin, spin, spin.
Here is the fly for the party.

Bee

Buzz, buzz, buzz.
Here is the nectar for the party.

Beetle
Butterfly will make the party pie.

Butterfly
In goes the lettuce leaf,
in goes the fly,
in goes the nectar,
for a sweet party pie.

The Butterfly Net

Written by Michele Ashley
Illustrated by Carol Herring

My brother said that he could get
A butterfly in his butterfly net.

My brother went out and he got set,
To catch a butterfly in his net.

I turned on the hose and he got wet!
So, no butterfly in his butterfly net.

readingsafari.com

Check out these Safari magazines, too!

Have your say -

e-mail your Safari Tour Guide at tourguide@readingsafari.com

Safari Tour Guide,

I have a garden of my own. Can I e-mail you a drawing of it?

Stevie Dobbs (6)

🌵 40

Find some fun things to do! Go to — http://www.readingsafari.com

Safari Superstar

Name – Beetle

Birthday – October 7

Find out more about this Safari Superstar at

http://www.readingsafari.com